WHAT READER

MW00685022

"*Build Your Business With Testimonials* was really awesome - easy to read, and definitely a page flipper. I had several a-ha's about where I could easily ask for testimonials. I especially liked the 6 questions to ask to create powerful testimonials. And I loved the distinction between feedback and testimonial. **There were *so* many ideas to leverage testimonials that you've got me excited about playing full out with this!** Thanks, Kathy, for this really priceless information. I look forward to sharing my results with you."

Adela M. Rubio, Energy Coach and Trainer
Rahway, New Jersey

"My favorite part was the 'Testimonials Snapshot' at the beginning and end of the book. It's such a great way to focus attention, and it was so much more fun to see it presented this way than, say, as a list of objectives. **I love the specific questions you used to draw out testimonials.** Thanks!"

Elizabeth Nofziger - Health, Fitness, and Life Balance Coach
Fresh Vision Coaching, Chicago, Illinois

"From Kathy's down-to-earth storytelling style, to her assessments, tips and examples, this book is a complete guide to success in building your business with testimonials.

I especially liked the chapter "Creating More Powerful Testimonials," a topic I bring up frequently with the entrepreneurs I coach. **This information is key in getting testimonials that will actually bring in business, and isn't that the point?"**

Lea Belair, PCC - Agent of the Future
Leap Coaching, Westford, Vermont

"I had lots of testimonials, but didn't know how to use them. **I feel confident that I can apply what I learned to effectively solicit and use testimonials to attract a new target market.** I also learned to appreciate and use the clients' own words, even if they seem quirky & unprofessional. One endorsement was 'She Rocks!' I now see the value of this very personal & heartfelt message!"

Linda Glass, Peacebuilders Consulting
Whitehorse, Yukon, Canada

"I felt like I was more informed about how to best acquire quality testimonials by asking the right questions and following up promptly. **I will begin gathering some great testimonials to launch my business**, using testimonials from other parts of my life that highlight appropriate skills and talents."

Stephanie Marisca, Program Director
Providence, Rhode Island

"**There's no wiggle room for excuses!** This book presents such a clear and compelling argument for using testimonials - and makes the process so straightforward and painless - that it's impossible to pretend that you can't easily do everything Kathy describes and have great testimonials for your business or services. The book made me feel like getting testimonials should be as natural as breathing."

Susan R. Meyer, Ed. D., CC
President, Life-Work Coach, Brooklyn, New York

BUILD YOUR BUSINESS WITH TESTIMONIALS

TEN STEPS TO MORE CLIENTS, MORE CUSTOMERS, MORE SALES

KATHY GULRICH

Copyright © 2006 by Kathy Gulrich. All rights reserved. No part of this book may be reproduced in any form, printed or electronic, without written permission from the author.

The smART logo is a trademark (TM) of Smart Business Coaching, New York, NY 10016.

Library of Congress Control Number: 2005910546

PCIP Publisher's Cataloging-In-Publication Data
(Prepared by The Donohue Group, Inc.)

Gulrich, Kathy.
    Build your business with testimonials : ten steps to more clients, more customers, more sales / Kathy Gulrich.

    p. ; cm.
    ISBN-13: 978-0-9746533-3-4
    ISBN-10: 0-9746533-3-0

1. Endorsements in advertising.   2. Business referrals.   3. Communication in marketing. 4. Marketing. 5. Small business--Management. I. Title.

HF5415.123 .G85 2006
658.802   2005910546

Center City Publishing
P.O. Box 1292
New York, NY 10156

"It is usually best to be generous with praise, but cautious with criticism."

Author Unknown

TABLE OF CONTENTS

FOREWORD

Kathy Gulrich's big idea is that building a business is fun. It's a message she shares in her coaching, training, and writing - and the approach she's used to grow her own business.

In *Build Your Business With Testimonials: Ten Steps to More Clients, More Customers, More Sales* she looks at one of the smartest ways to build business credibility. Then she walks you through an easy-to-follow process that literally sparks you into action.

"Why haven't I been doing this?" I wondered with every page turn. The steps are so logical and painless the only reasonable response is to follow them.

In the years I have known Kathy, she's coached me into a bolder approach to my business, then helped me break it into manageable chunks. Her ability to "push without pushing" shows up just as strongly on the printed page.

An experienced marketing professional, Kathy knows her stuff and translates it into clear, practical information framed with steps we can follow. She makes getting and using testimonials look like fun. And, you'll discover, it is fun. Credibility and confidence are valuable side effects.

In my work counselling business people on mission-critical communication, key rules are: "Help people care," and, "Help people trust you." In selling products or ideas, the switch that turns on someone's decision to buy is likely to be emotional, rather than logical. Testimonials let you move potential buyers in the direction of trust and caring - using the heartfelt praise of people who clearly believe in what you're offering.

I encourage you to read *Build Your Business With Testimonials* and to follow its advice. Then make room for more business.

Sue Johnston, MBA, ABC
Consultant, Trainer, Coach
It's Understood Communication
Ottawa, Canada
www.itsunderstood.com

A long-time communication specialist and business writer, Sue is an Accredited Business Communicator and Chair of the Canada East Region of the International Association of Business Communicators (IABC). Her upcoming book on improving personal and corporate performance through effective face-to-face communication is scheduled for release later this year.

INTRODUCTION

I did my first testimonials because ... well ... I had no choice.

I was a copywriter in a New York advertising agency, working on a farm chemicals account. Our advertising budget got cut drastically. And that meant no new TV commercials for the next growing season.

So my photographer and I headed across the country to meet with farmers who were using our products - and to tape interviews that we could use to create a much less expensive radio and magazine ad campaign.

Several weeks later, listening to the interviews again in my high-rise Manhattan office, I was blown away by what I heard.

It wasn't so much what the farmers said, but how they said it. They spoke with conviction - clearly from a place of knowledge and experience. Every interview flowed with the rhythms of regional dialect, personal anecdotes, touches of humor. Man, these guys were so real!

This authenticity translated beautifully into our testimonial-based radio commercials. They really struck a chord with other farmers - and totally out-performed our previous TV advertising, at a fraction of the cost.

I became a believer.

Having been thrown into testimonials without a whit of experience, I realized that there was a lot to learn. There's some good news, however: When you get right down to it, getting great testimonials is actually pretty easy. And learning to use testimonials to your best advantage isn't all that difficult - if you follow a few simple steps.

And that's what this book is all about.

Stick with it, and before you know it you, too, will have powerful testimonials that will attract new customers and clients to your business.

Kathy Gulrich

YOUR "TESTIMONIALS SNAPSHOT"

To get a snapshot of the progress you've made so far in using testimonials, please take a few minutes to rate yourself on each of the following topics, using this rating scale:

1 - I have no idea how to do this
2 - I understand this, but haven't yet started
3 - I've got a pretty good start
4 - I've done it, but would like to improve
5 - I'm a pro!

Not where you'd like to be in every area? No problem. Look to the right of the checklist, and you'll find out where you can learn more.

						Learn More In
I always ask for feedback immediately following my programs and events	1	2	3	4	5	Chapter 2
I routinely request testimonials or endorsements from leaders in my field	1	2	3	4	5	Chapter 2

						Learn More In
I quickly follow up on unsolicited feedback to get necessary permissions	*1*	*2*	*3*	*4*	*5*	*Chapter 2*
I know how to use offers to get more feedback, more testimonials	*1*	*2*	*3*	*4*	*5*	*Chapter 3*
I have a great list of questions that help me get powerful testimonials	*1*	*2*	*3*	*4*	*5*	*Chapter 4*
I know how to choose – and edit – testimonials to build my business	*1*	*2*	*3*	*4*	*5*	*Chapter 6*
I get proper permission for every testimonial – whether I'm ready to use it, or not	*1*	*2*	*3*	*4*	*5*	*Chapter 5*
I collect all the contact information I need to make the testimonial credible	*1*	*2*	*3*	*4*	*5*	*Chapter 5*
I understand how and where to use testimonials in my marketing materials	*1*	*2*	*3*	*4*	*5*	*Chapters 6, 7*
I regularly write endorsements and testimonials for others' products	*1*	*2*	*3*	*4*	*5*	*Chapter 8*

CHAPTER ONE: THE POWER OF TESTIMONIALS

How effective are testimonials in getting new clients and customers? You can answer this one for yourself.

Before you purchased your last book, did you flip to the back cover to read what other people had to say about it? Did you ask for references before hiring your last employee, or consultant? Read the testimonials on the last website you visited? Or check out what people had to say about me before you purchased this book?

Chances are you've read this far because you read testimonials yourself. Yes, you're turned off by testimonials that sound false. But you're moved one step closer to purchase by testimonials that strike a chord, or touch on something that's really important to you.

Let's get started by taking a look at some good business reasons to use testimonials.

What's in it for you?

Ah, now this question is fairly straightforward. You might use testimonials because:

- Testimonials are much more believable, more credible, than advertising
- They can be used to say things about you, or your products and services, that you could never say yourself
- They resonate with your prospects
- Testimonials give people a reason to do business with you
- Your testimonial writers will uncover, and then point out, some 'off-the-beaten-track' benefits of your products or services

And did you know that people who write testimonials for you often become your most loyal, long-term customers? Here are a few reasons why they stay:

- They're flattered you asked their opinion
- They stay by virtue of the fact that they've already said you're great
- They feel part of building your business, so they hang around to see how it develops

Are you ready to give testimonials a try? Now for the next question....

What's in it for them?

Yes, this is a slightly tougher question. To answer it, put yourself in the shoes of someone who's thinking of writing you a testimonial. What do they get out of writing it?

- To start, they get the satisfaction of helping you out
- In writing the testimonial, they review everything they've gained in working with you, or using your product - this in itself is of value to them
- They get recognition by being listed on your website, or in your brochure or advertisement
- And they may even get more business - since readers may follow the link from your site (or advertising) directly to them, their company, and their products

So, the next time you're a bit hesitant about asking for a testimonial, look back at this list. You'll be reminded how the person you're asking will benefit, too.

TIP: Are you relatively new to testimonials? One of the fastest ways to learn more is to check out how other people are using them. Head to the websites of the leaders in your field, and see what they're up to. What might also work for you?

CHAPTER TWO: THE BASICS

If you want great testimonials, you have to ask for them. Usually, that is. As you'll learn in the second step in this chapter, you may already have testimonials tucked away that you haven't even considered. For all testimonials, however, it's all about timing.

STEP 1: Ask for testimonials often, and immediately.

You can never have too many testimonials.

Make it a habit: Ask for feedback, endorsements, and testimonials for virtually everything you do:

- Products
- Services
- Speaking engagements
- Consultations
- Individual coaching
- Teleclasses
- Trainings

Who are the "famous" people you'd like to write a testimonial for you? Ask them!

And remember, you don't need to offer a paid product or service in order to ask for a testimonial. Do you offer free samples, or free introductory sessions? Do you lead free teleclasses? These are terrific opportunities for great testimonials. In fact, by virtue of the fact that you're offering your time or product at no charge, your audience may be even more willing to help you out.

Ask for testimonials immediately after - or even before - the event, or the product launch.

Strike while the iron's hot.

I've found that waiting more than a couple of days after an event to ask for feedback significantly lowers the number of responses I get back. So don't wait!

- If you're doing a live event, hand out your feedback form on the spot - perhaps at the back of the room, or along with the presentation materials

- For virtual events (teleclasses, webinars, etc.), send out your e-mail request for testimonials within a day or so

- Add a feedback form to your website or blog so that people can write their comments - and see them posted online - almost instantaneously

Are you ready to be bold? Ask for testimonals before your product or service launches:

- Send a free sample of your product (your new book, for example) to leaders in your field, or other experts or potential users, and ask for a pre-publication or pre-launch testimonial

- If you have an upcoming live workshop or seminar, you can often get pre-event testimonials by forwarding your workshop notes or outline to business contacts or colleagues for review

Remember to give your reviewers enough time! A close colleague might be able to read your seminar outline and get you a written review in a few days. On the other hand, you'll generally need to allow two to three months for a busy, well-known author or expert in your field to read a pre-publication copy of your book and respond.

TIP: Even if you're starting a brand new business, or dramatically changing the focus of your existing business, all you need is a bit of creativity to get effective testimonials for your new endeavor. Here are a couple of suggestions to get you started:

- Get testimonials on the **talents and skills** that translate well into your new business or niche - for example, a brand new coach has probably coached their friends or colleagues 'unofficially' (guiding, supporting, helping build strategies, etc.) long before they started their coaching business

- Capitalize on the **similar needs of diverse target groups** - for example, if you've been doing great financial planning for teachers, and are just beginning to work with dentists, you could use testimonials from your existing teacher clients in your new materials

Tap your network, ask your friends, look at your past customers. With just a bit of creativity - and persistence - you'll be able to get several credible testimonials well in advance of your new business launch.

STEP 2: Be on the lookout for unsolicited testimonials.

Okay, this one's my favorite. It's just so easy!

I'd be willing to bet that you're already getting lots of unsolicited, spontaneous testimonials. All you need to do in order to master this step is get into the habit of noticing them.

Check your e-mail:

How often does someone write a quick e-mail to thank you for your terrific class or workshop? Or to let you know how much they enjoyed reading your newsletter? Or to thank you for responding to them so quickly?

These are testimonials in the making. Simply shoot back an e-mail - the same day - that thanks them for their comments, and asks permission to use what they wrote as a testimonial.

Here's one way to do it:

Sample e-mail:

> Kathy, I'd love to use some of your kind words from your e-mail as a testimonial at some point - on my website, or in my marketing materials.
>
> I'd usually include your comments with your name and location, something like this:
>
> Kathy Gulrich, smART Business Coaching
> New York, NY
> www.smARTbusinessCoaching.com
>
> Would that be okay? If so, please let me know by return e-mail. Thanks.
>
> Meanwhile, I look forward to hearing more about how this class impacts your business. Please keep me posted.
>
> Warmly,
> Your Name

Note: If their e-mail was missing any critical information (for example, their website address) now is the time to ask for it. In the sample above, you might use www.YourWebsite.com as a place-holder, and revise the text slightly, like this:

"Would that be okay? If so, please let me know your website address if you have one (or when you get one), so that people who read your testimonial can link back to your site. Thanks."

Listen with a 'new' ear at business events:

Have you ever been at a networking or business event when someone made a point of telling you how much they enjoyed your book, or seminar, or teleclass, or...? (Yep, another testimonial opportunity!)

This is a little bit trickier, since you're speaking, and testimonials are generally written. It's still a great opportunity, if you take advantage of it. Here are two ways to move the process forward:

- Let them know you're flattered, and that you'd love to have them write down their thoughts for you to use as a written testimonial. Give them your business card along with your thanks; and be sure to follow up with a reminder (e-mail, if appropriate) the next morning.

- Tell them that what they're saying would be perfect for a testimonial, and ask them if it would be okay for you to jot down a few notes while you're chatting. Let them know that you'll write up what they said, and send it to them for approval in the morning.

Sample e-mails:
First scenario:

Kathy, it was great to meet you at the conference dinner last evening. Thanks again for your perspectives and feedback on my book, *Build Your Business With Testimonials*.

I really appreciate your support and, as I mentioned last night, I'd love to have you put your insights into writing (informally is great!) so that I can use them as a testimonial at some point - on my website, or in my marketing materials. Thanks again for your kind offer to write them.

When you get back to me, please also verify your contact information (full name, title, company, city/state, and website address) so that I'll be able to include it with your testimonial - so that my readers can also support you.

Thanks again, Kathy.

Warmly,
Your Name

Second scenario:

Kathy, it was great to meet you at the conference dinner last evening. Thanks again for your perspectives and feedback on my book, *Build Your Business With Testimonials*

I really appreciate your support and, as I mentioned last night, I'd love to be able to use your insights as a testimonial at some point - on my website, or in my marketing materials.

I've written up what you shared with me, and included it below. Please feel free to change anything I misunderstood, or that doesn't work for you - and add anything else that feels appropriate. Thanks.

Please also verify that your contact information (also below) is correct so that my readers will be able to learn more about you.

If you have any questions, please let me know. I look forward to hearing back from you soon!

Warmly,
Your Name

CHAPTER THREE: GETTING MORE TESTIMONIALS

Follow the guidelines in Chapters 1 and 2, and you'll have plenty of testimonials. Follow the guidelines in this Chapter, and you'll have even more. Just two steps, both simple.

STEP 3: *Offer something in exchange for feedback.*

There's no question that offers work. Think of your own experience: You're not sure you need that new shirt, but it's 30% off today. You'll purchase the tennis racquet at full price, *if* the pro throws in a can of balls. You may even be tempted to order a drink with that burger in order to get the free side of fries. Offers work.

The trick with testimonials is to find an offer that's appealing, but doesn't feel like a 'bribe.' For each item in the list below, decide whether you would feel comfortable making that offer to your potential buyers, or customers. For any offer that is not okay with you, write what bothers you about it - and what you might offer instead.

Offer	OK	If you wouldn't use the offer, why not? How could you change it to make it work for you?
I'd appreciate it if you'd please read this new article, and provide me with your feedback. As a thank you, I'll send you a link to my article archive page.		
If you're willing to provide feedback for me, I'll be happy to send you a complimentary copy of my upcoming book.		
I'm hoping to add new testimonials to my website. If you'd be willing to contribute some thoughts based on your experience with my company, I'll be happy to provide you with a complimentary one-hour business analysis.		
I'd appreciate it if you'd send me your feedback on my soon-to-be-published book. When it's printed, I'll feature your testimonial prominently on the back cover.		
Simply send me your testimonial, and I'll send you a $20-off coupon good for your next purchase.		
I hope you enjoyed this workshop, and look forward to hearing your feedback. If you respond before next Friday, I'll send you a coupon for $100 savings on any upcoming workshop.		

When you're creating - or evaluating - your offers, one thing to think about is how well the offer matches what you're asking someone to do. For example, if you're just asking someone to take a quick glance at your article, offering an hour-long consultation as a thank-you would probably be out of balance.

TIP: Use deadlines to get people into action. Ever wonder why so many offers say "limited time only" or "respond by midnight Thursday?" Quite simply, because deadlines work.

When choosing a deadline, make it slightly challenging ... but attainable. The purpose is to kick someone into action, now - and to push them through that "should I, shouldn't I" decision.

Important: If you give a deadline, enforce it! Let it slip, and your credibility will slip right along with it.

STEP 4: *Make it easy.*

Many marketers think that saying, simply, "Could you please write me a testimonial?" makes it easier for the person they're asking to write it. It's not.

Fact is, it's pretty tough to write anything without some structure. Asking a few specific questions - or letting your customer know exactly what kind of information you're looking for - will actually make it much easier for them. (Check out some sample questions in Chapter Four, next.)

Do you have a customer or client who could use even more help?

Consider writing the testimonial for them.

If someone you know really supports your business, or your product, but is hesitant to write a testimonial for you, ask yourself why.

If your gut tells you that for some reason they'd prefer not to make a public endorsement of your product, leave it at that. Honor their wishes and their privacy.

There could be other reasons you sense some hesitation, however. Perhaps they're simply too busy to take on an extra task. Or perhaps they're a bit insecure about their writing ability, and don't want to disappoint you. In these cases, you might offer to write the testimonial for them. Here's how:

- Interview them about their experience with your product or service (you might use the questions in Chapter Four as your guide)

- Write up your notes - including all the main points they made, and using as much of their language as possible

- Submit your notes to them for any editing that's needed, and their approval (the last sample e-mail in Chapter Two may help you with this)

CHAPTER FOUR: CREATING MORE POWERFUL TESTIMONIALS

So far, we've looked at lots of tools and techniques you can use to get *more* testimonials, from more people and more places. This chapter will show you how to make sure that every testimonial you get will work hard to build your business.

STEP 5: Ask specific questions.

Feel free to use the following questions exactly as written, or tailor them to fit your business. I suggest you keep the overall structure of the questions the same, however. By asking all six questions, you'll get testimonials that cover virtually all aspects of your product or service. Even better, they'll likely be in the real 'language' of the writer - which will resonate with readers, and lead to sales.

So, the questions - along with brief notes about why they're included, or written in this format. Here we go:

1 - Why did you seek out my product/service? What were you hoping to improve, or resolve?

(With this question, you'll find out which issues are most often encountered by your target market. Two benefits here. First, you'll get more insight on what drives your customers to you and your products. And the issues mentioned in the testimonials will resonate with others in your target market.)

2 - How do you feel as a result?

("Feel" is the most important word in this question; don't change it! This question leads to testimonials that will include emotion, and cause readers to connect with what's written.)

3 - What concept or idea in the product/presentation helped you most? How so?

(Answers to this question will elicit testimonials on several different aspects of your product, presentation, or service - which will help you 'cover all the bases' when you use your testimonials.)

4 - How are you currently using what you learned?

(In a nutshell, this makes it real - and therefore much more powerful.)

5 - What specific results did you get? Any surprises?

(Yes, asking for 'specific' results will get you much stronger/more credible testimonials. And the "surprises" part of this question opens it up for unique or interesting comments you wouldn't have thought to ask about!)

6 - What would you like to say to someone who is considering purchasing this product/using this service?

(Answers to this question are often very powerful when used on your website, or in your brochure, near where you ask for the sale.)

TIP: If there's something in particular that you'd like to get across to potential buyers or clients, ask a question that is likely to elicit a testimonial on that subject.

For example, if having testimonials about my writing ability were important to me, I might add one of these questions to the list above:

- "How did Kathy's writing style contribute to your learning?"

- "Would you say that Kathy's writing style made your learning easier? More interesting? Something else? Be as specific as you can, please."

CHAPTER FIVE: THE FINE PRINT

I promise, this will be the only chapter filled with 'fine print.' And I'll keep it short.

STEP 6: Get permission - and all the information you need.

It's simply not okay - or legal, for that matter - to use someone's testimonial without their express, written permission. Whether you consult with your attorney (recommended!), or decide to create your own permission form, be sure it includes the following:

- Date

- Copy of the text/testimonial itself

- Permission to edit as needed: to "use all or in part" or to "edit for space"

- Permission for "any and all uses"

- Permission to use the person's name, title, company, etc. along with their testimonial

Clearly, a signed and dated consent form from the writer is best. Many marketers use a return e-mail indicating the writer's permission as the consent form. Either way, be sure to file away both the testimonial - and the writer's permission to use it - in a safe place.

Increase credibility.

Your testimonials will be much more believable if they come along with robust information about the person who wrote them. Consider the following choices. Which are you most likely to believe?

"I learned so much from *Build Your Business With Testimonials* that I'm recommending it to all of my clients and colleagues."
K.G., Coach in New York

"I learned so much from *Build Your Business With Testimonials* that I'm recommending it to all of my clients and colleagues."
    Kathy Gulrich, Coach
    smART Business Coaching, New York, NY
    www.smARTbusinessCoaching.com

Also be sure to get all the contact or business information you'll need right away - when you're asking for permission to use the testimonial. Ask for (and confirm spellings for!) any or all of the following that you think you might use with your testimonials now, or in the future:

- Full name
- City, State
- Country
- Company Name
- Job Title
- Website Address
- E-mail Address
- Telephone (with city/country codes)
- Credentials (M.Ed., MCC, etc.)
- Photograph
- Audio or Video Clip

TIP: While you're asking for contact information, credentials, and approval, be sure to *thank the person who wrote the testimonial for you!*

CHAPTER SIX: CHOOSING YOUR TESTIMONIALS

By now you probably have more testimonials than you can use. Great! That puts you in an enviable position: You're able to sort through all the testimonials you have, and come up with a short list of testimonials that will work extremely hard for you. In this chapter, some guidelines for finding the 'best of the best.'

STEP 7: Be extremely selective.

Whenever you use testimonials in your marketing, you have the opportunity to select them - and edit them - in a way that will make them even more powerful. Use your gut, and follow your intuition. What you feel from the testimonial is almost always more important, and more powerful, than the facts that are included.

That said, here are some practical suggestions to keep in mind:

If it's not fabulous, don't use it.

Not everyone will agree with me when I say it's better to have no testimonials at all, than to use weak or unbelievable testimonials. Trust your feelings about this. My thoughts: You'll have the opportunity to get better and better testimonials as you introduce new products, develop new services, and build your business. Don't be over-anxious. Only use testimonials that truly support your business.

Keep testimonials clear and concise.

Okay, for some audiences - or for extremely complicated products and services - long, detailed testimonials may actually make sense. In most cases, however, a clear, concise testimonial (about 2-5 sentences long) will do the job for you. If the testimonial goes on, and on, and on ... cut!

Don't lose the 'flavor' of the writer.

Very often, the quirky or slightly odd phrases that someone uses in writing the testimonial are the very words that will make a special connection with the reader. Don't be tempted to edit them out. Keep the testimonial in the writer's own words.

Edit your testimonials to highlight your key selling points.

Very few testimonials arrive to us in perfect shape for publication. They're often too long, or very repetitive. They might ramble on a bit. And sometimes testimonials include so many benefits that they end up being confusing. That's where great editing comes in. These two simple editing techniques may help:

- Limit each testimonial to one major benefit, or key selling point. Include additional information only if it clearly supports your key message.

- Use bold type to pull readers into your testimonials - and to draw their attention to the particular words or phrases that best support your product or service.

To illustrate how you might do this, I've included an example below. In the first section, you'll see a testimonial that I received from one of my "Ask Kathy Live" participants. In the boxes that follow, I'll show you several different ways that you might edit this very long feedback into several shorter, better focused, testimonials.

The long version...

Kathy, I wanted to take a moment to thank you for taking your valuable time to do "Ask Kathy Live." My schedule on Thursdays is now organized around the conference call with you and all the other artists who show up for the call. Initially I didn't know what to expect but I realized quickly that I had to take advantage of the opportunity. Whether I have a question of my own or I just listen to other artists, I learn something useful on each call.

Since I started the weekly calls to "Ask Kathy Live," I have been inspired to enjoy the business of art. I enjoy communicating with other artists I would otherwise not know or speak with. I also enjoy knowing that I am not the only one who needs a little advice and encouragement. I have always known it wasn't enough to simply be creative if I wanted to be a professional artist and thrive from my craft. The only question I really had was, where do I go to get this info I so desperately need? I guess the universe or God or whomever you believe in finally heard me asking and sent me in the right direction, "Ask Kathy Live."

I enjoy calling in each week because it keeps me fresh. It reminds me of things I still need to take care of, even if we don't discuss it. It's my weekly artist check in. By implementing thoughts and ideas I have received not only from you, but other artists on the call, I have improved every aspect of my artist career. I've set goals and met a majority of them already. I am more organized and thus more inspired to be true to myself as an artist. There is no hesitation to announce to the world "Yes indeed, I am an Artist!" It's no longer a second thought in how I express myself to others. Art is not my favorite pastime, it's who I am, and I feel much more confident to express that to anyone and everyone.

I enjoy being a part of something that is positive, encouraging and educational. I don't know if making the call came just in time to meet a need, or if because I made the call I realized what I needed. Either way, I am now more excited then scared. I have comfort in knowing when I move on to the next step, if I can't figure out what I am doing or how to do it, when I call "Ask Kathy Live" on Thursday, Kathy will help me discover options to manage the challenge.

I am very thankful for all your input. I just put up a new web page yesterday to let people know where I am showing my artwork. I have a show in San Ramon, California in a few weeks. Two pieces were accepted, and I have the option to send a third if it is related to their theme.

Thank you for dedicating your valuable time to those of us who need you, and otherwise might not be able to afford personal coaching at this time. You are making a difference and I am inspired.

Valarie Love, Artist
Jacksonville, FL
www.valarielovesart.com

Question: Did you read the entire testimonial? Most readers will not. They'll read the first paragraph or two ... skim very quickly over the rest of the text ... and then look to see what's at the very end. (That's one of the reasons that I prefer using short testimonials.)

There are many different ways to make several shorter, more powerful testimonials from the long text above. Some might highlight product benefits, while others focus on results. How do you decide? Simply keep your marketing and sales objectives in mind, and experiment until you end up with something that resonates for you.

Here are a few samples to give you an idea of how I might go about it:

Example 1. Objective: Make fine artists comfortable with the idea of a teleclass/conference call

"My schedule on Thursdays is now organized around the conference call with you and all the other artists who show up for "Ask Kathy Live." Initially, I didn't know what to expect. But I realized quickly that I had to take advantage of the opportunity. **Whether I have a question of my own, or I just listen to other artists, I learn something useful on each call**. I enjoy communicating with other artists I would otherwise not know or speak with. It's also great to know that I am not the only one who needs a little advice and encouragement."

Valarie Love, Artist
Jacksonville, FL
www.valarielovesart.com

Example 2. Objective: Highlight how the calls support the business side of art.

"Since I started the weekly calls to "Ask Kathy Live," I have been inspired to enjoy the business of art. By implementing thoughts and ideas I have received from you - and from the other artists on the call - **I have improved every aspect of my artist career**. I've set goals and met a majority of them already. I enjoy calling in each week because it keeps me fresh. It's my weekly artist check in."

Valarie Love, Artist
Jacksonville, FL
www.valarielovesart.com

Example 3. Objective: Focus on specific, measurable results.

"I am very thankful for all your input on the "Ask Kathy Live" calls. I just put up a new web page yesterday to let people know where I am showing my artwork. **I have a show in San Ramon, California in a few weeks.** Two pieces were accepted, and I have the option to send a third if it is related to their theme. I have comfort in knowing when I move on to the next step, if I can't figure out what I am doing or how to do it, you will help me discover options to manage the challenge."

Valarie Love, Artist
Jacksonville, FL
www.valarielovesart.com

Example 4. Objective: Promote Kathy as a warm, caring coach.

"I enjoy being a part of something that is positive, encouraging and educational. I don't know if making the call came just in time to meet a need, or if because I made the call I realized what I needed. Either way, I am now more excited then scared. Thank you for dedicating your valuable time to those of us who need you, and otherwise might not be able to afford personal coaching at this time. **You are making a difference, and I am inspired.**"

Valarie Love, Artist
Jacksonville, FL
www.valarielovesart.com

Example 5. Objective: Focus on personal/emotional results.

"I enjoy calling in to "Ask Kathy Live" each week because it keeps me fresh. I am more organized and thus more inspired to be true to myself as an artist. **There is no hesitation to announce to the world, "Yes indeed, I am an Artist!"** There's no second thought about how I express myself to others. Art is not my favorite pastime, it's who I am, and I feel much more confident to express that to anyone and everyone."

Valarie Love, Artist
Jacksonville, FL
www.valarielovesart.com

CHAPTER SEVEN: USING TESTIMONIALS FOR RESULTS

Some of the work you did around objectives (Chapter 6) will make it clear where particular testimonials will have the most impact. But while there are guidelines, exactly how or where to use testimonials is more of an art than a science. The word of the day: Experiment.

STEP 8: Include testimonials wherever you ask for action.

Let's talk websites first. There are a few places on our websites where most of us ask our visitors to take action. You can strategically use testimonials at - or leading up to - these "action points:"

- Home page - where we ask visitors to keep reading, and move to other pages on our site

- Newsletter sign-up page - where we ask visitors to write their names and contact information

- Consultation or Sales Call sign-up page - again, where we ask for contact information

- Order pages(s) - where we ask people to part with their money; to purchase our product or service

The same holds true for brochures: Your brochure cover, or intro page, is where you ask your readers to open the brochure, and read further. Why not start with a testimonial? Similarly, you might include a testimonial on the page where you ask someone to call you or take another action, say, fill out a coupon.

Doing a one-page advertisement? Think about using a testimonial near the top, to capture the reader's interest, then another near your coupon, or toll-free number. Whatever your marketing method, think "action points," and you'll be on a great path.

The long and the short of it.

There's some question about which works best: Many relatively short testimonials woven throughout the text, or a testimonial "section" where readers, if interested, can find all of your testimonials, in full length.

Truth is, there's no "right" answer. Personally? I seldom read long testimonials; so I'm quite happy running into many short ones interspersed throughout the website, or brochure. What do you think your target audience will respond to? What feels right to you?

TIP: On your website, you can have the best of both worlds: Include short testimonials in several places, and end each with a "click here to read more" link to the longer version for those who are interested in learning more. And if you're really uncomfortable breaking up your text with testimonials, don't! Instead, add a "What people are saying about us" link to your navigation bar, and put all your testimonials on that page.

Choose testimonials that illustrate just the right things.

What are "just the right things?" Good question. You'll find the answer by thinking carefully about what you're trying to accomplish by including testimonials on your website, or in your other marketing materials. Your objectives might include:

- Make a sale

- Get someone to sign up for your newsletter

- Encourage someone to read more about your business

- Point out a particular benefit of your product/service (easy to use, saves you time/money, only product on the market that will solve this problem for you, etc.)

- Point out how your product/service out-performs the competition

- Show a variety of different reasons for choosing your product/service

- Illustrate how your product/service works well with many different audiences

- Show that you have well-established, well-known endorsers

- Point out one - or more - of your talents/abilities (great writer, compassionate, marketing expert, etc.)

- Anything else?

In addition to helping ensure that your testimonials cover all the bases - thinking "objectives" will help you decide where to use which testimonial in your marketing materials.

Partner testimonials with your key points, and your marketing objectives.

If you select - and edit - your testimonials carefully, you'll end up with a large selection of testimonials that each speak clearly to one or more of your product benefits. When you're organizing your website or brochure, make note of the key concept, selling point, or marketing objective for each page or section - then simply add the testimonial that fits best, and best illustrates the concept. (You'll find examples of how to edit testimonials in Chapter 6.)

TIP: When filing away paper copies of my testimonials, I've found it very helpful to organize them (along with the accompanying permissions, of course) into broad areas: Newsletter, Coaching, Teleclasses, Live Workshops/Seminars, my Book, CD, Article Series, etc.

Then, on each printout, I make a quick note that reminds me - without having to re-read the testimonial - the major benefit(s) or area(s) covered. These notes are very informal snippets. For a marketing teleclass, for example, my notes might include: "first teleclass ever, surprised at how effective," "thought TC was clear/understandable," "likes my teaching style; interactive class," "using my checklist with his clients," etc.

Keep those testimonials moving.

You may remember that I mentioned "experiment" at the beginning of the chapter. That's because experimenting - to find out what works, and what doesn't - will have an incredibly positive impact on the results you'll get from your testimonials. And experimenting is very easy to do on your website.

How do you find out what's working?

- You can learn a lot from your site stats (have a chat with your web host, or website designer, if you don't already have access to these)

- You'll know what's working by noticing how adding (or changing, or removing) a testimonial affects your product sales ... or consultation sign-ups ... or coupon returns ... or newsletter subscriptions

51

- And don't forget the obvious: Ask your prospects and customers what they think - which testimonials they've noticed, which they think are the most powerful, most accurate, most believable, etc.

Finally, keep it fresh! Change out your testimonials every few months or so - or more frequently, if you get a lot of repeat traffic to your website. Even if your site content remains relatively unchanged, new testimonials will make your website feel fresh - and give visitors the impression that you always have something new and exciting to tell them about.

CHAPTER EIGHT: MORE BANG FOR YOUR MARKETING BUCK

Yes, testimonials are an incredibly powerful marketing tool. Yes, they'll build credibility for your products and services. And yes, they'll give your prospects yet another good reason to do business with you. But that's just the beginning, actually.

STEP 9: Leverage your testimonials.

So far, we've been focusing on using testimonials on your website, and in marketing brochures or advertisements. Don't let this limit your creativity in using testimonials! You might also include testimonials in (or on) your:

- Business Card
- E-mail Signature
- Article Bio
- Joint Endorsement Mailings
- e-Product, or Book: Introductory pages - and back cover
- e-Product, or Book: Use testimonials as illustrations or relevant quotations within your document

And to get even more clients and customers interested in your business, think of testimonials much more broadly....

- Think "feedback" vs. "testimonial" and you have a whole new - and totally free - market research tool; a great way to learn more

- How about creating market surveys with a double objective: Answering your marketing questions and providing testimonials or endorsements for your business

- Might you be able to use this market research - with testimonials included - as part of a new product? Or as a free report?

- Consider inviting everyone who has written you a testimonial to a special teleclass or seminar (what fun!)

- Ask people who have already sent you a testimonial for your book to write a review on amazon.com, or on other websites where your book is sold

- Encourage your testimonial writers to recommend your product or service to their friends and colleagues (setting up an Affiliate Program will give them even more incentive to follow through)

Get creative. Think collaboration. How else might you leverage testimonials in your business?

STEP 10: *Write testimonials yourself. Lots of them.*

"Walk the talk," I say!

If you ask your customers for testimonials, please also be willing to provide testimonials for products, services, and businesses that you use and like. When you write them, take the time and effort to do a great job. And be sure to include your full name, along with your credentials, contact information, website address, and so on - so that people can link from the other websites back to you.

One caveat, however: Never, never endorse a product or service that you haven't actually used - or that you're not totally enthusiastic about. Your positive words about a ho-hum (or worse, defective or unprofessional) product will instantly damage your credibility with your customers and prospects. Sometimes irreparably so.

READY FOR ACTION!

Now that you've finished the book, I hope you'll please take a few minutes to rate yourself once again on each of the following topics - so that you can see how much you've learned:

1 - I have no idea how to do this
2 - I understand this, but haven't yet started
3 - I've got a pretty good start
4 - I've done it, but would like to improve
5 - I'm a pro!

I will always ask for feedback immediately following my programs and events	1	2	3	4	5
I have the confidence to request testimonials from leaders in my field	1	2	3	4	5
I know how to follow up on unsolicited feedback to get necessary permissions	1	2	3	4	5
I know how to use offers to get more feedback, more testimonials	1	2	3	4	5
I have a great list of questions that will help me get powerful testimonials	1	2	3	4	5

I know how to choose – and edit – testimonials to build my business	1	2	3	4	5
I will get proper permission for every testimonial – whether I'm ready to use it, or not	1	2	3	4	5
I will collect all the contact information I need to make my testimonials credible	1	2	3	4	5
I understand how and where to use testimonials in my marketing materials	1	2	3	4	5
I will write endorsements and testimonials for others' products often	1	2	3	4	5

So, how did you do? See any changes for the positive? On a scale of 1-10, how confident are you that you can now get - and use - testimonials effectively?

WHAT'S NEXT?

First, thank you for purchasing *Build Your Business With Testimonials: Ten Steps to More Clients, More Customers, More Sales*. And thanks for the time you spent with me exploring this one corner of the fabulous world of marketing (one of my great passions).

I really hope you've come away with lots of ideas and practical tips that you will put into action to build your business.

Would you like to have the *Ten Steps* all in one place, for quick reference? (I thought so.)

STEP 1: Ask for testimonials often, and immediately.

STEP 2: Be on the lookout for unsolicited testimonials.

STEP 3: Offer something in exchange for feedback.

STEP 4: Make it easy.

STEP 5: Ask specific questions.

STEP 6: Get permission - and all the information you need.

STEP 7: Be extremely selective.

STEP 8: Include testimonials wherever you ask for action.

STEP 9: Leverage your testimonials.

STEP 10: Write testimonials yourself. Lots of them.

One last word: Remember, all the steps and tips and ideas in this book can't do a thing to build your business unless you actually use them. So I heartily encourage you to turn your new-found knowledge and enthusiasm into action - now - so you, too, will soon see great results from testimonials.

ABOUT THE AUTHOR

In a nutshell, Kathy will help you build your business - and have fun in the process.

She'll start by helping you get projects off the back burner, and into action. How? She breaks it all down into simple, easy-to-follow steps - then adds her ongoing structure and support. She especially likes business-building projects that include writing and marketing. (When you meet her, you'll see: She loves this stuff!)

Kathy knows how to get things done! And her clients love her direct, no-nonsense approach.

Kathy brings nearly twenty years experience as teacher, corporate trainer, and workshop leader to her coaching business. And she often draws on the marketing skills she gained in her 15+ years as Creative Director for leading advertising agencies in New York, Hong Kong, Singapore, and Milan..

Her passion for writing, teaching, and marketing found a happy home when she joined CoachVille three years ago. Kathy is currently Community Coach of the 'Mastering Change' learning community, and an instructor in CoachVille's innovative new Graduate School of Coaching.

She has earned a couple of degrees (B.A. from Rutgers University in New Jersey, and her M.Ed. from West Chester College, Pennsylvania). She's a member of the International Association of Coaches, and the International Coach Federation. And Kathy is also a successful author (her first book for artists quickly became an amazon.com best-seller).

Today, you'll most often find Kathy working out of her office - and art studio - located in a beautiful 150-year-old brownstone in midtown Manhattan.

YOUR FEEDBACK, PLEASE

I hope you'll please take a few minutes to share your feedback on *Build Your Business With Testimonials: Ten Steps to More Clients, More Customers, More Sales.* I'd really like to know what you think.

When writing your comments, please feel free to use the questions I suggested in Chapter Four as a guide (you'll find them on pages 32 and 33).

And when you send them to me,* please indicate that you give permission for me to use the information you provided - including your name and contact information - as a testimonial on my website or in my other marketing materials. Please know that I may edit your feedback for space, or for a particular use.

Most often, your testimonial will appear along with your name, company, and website address, so that others may link back to your website - and learn more about your products and services. So please also include:

Your full name
Job title
Credentials (M.Ed., MCC, etc.)
Company Name
City, State, Country

Website address
E-mail address

Thanks so much for taking the time to provide your feedback on this project. I really appreciate it.

As a special thank you, I'll be happy to send you the link to a recording of a recent teleclass I led on testimonials (when you send your feedback to me, simply indicate code TC03 in your letter or e-mail;* thanks). Perhaps listening to the class will give you a few new ideas - and inspire you even further to get started using testimonials in your business.

Let's create more success!
Kathy

I look forward to hearing from you:
via e-mail: kathy@smARTbusinessCoaching.com
by mail: Kathy Gulrich, Center City Publishing, P.O. Box 1292, New York, NY 10156